Crushed *but not* Forsaken

God's Promises to the Widow, the Fatherless, and the Hurting

Dr. Robert White

Copyright © 2009 Dr. Robert White
All rights reserved.

ISBN: 1-4392-6517-8
ISBN-13: 9781439265178

DEDICATION

The writing of this book would not have been possible without the loving support of my precious wife, the prayerful support of my godly Mom, the encouraging support of my brothers and sisters in Christ and the unfailing support of my great Savior.

This book is dedicated to all those who seek a deeper, more intimate walk with the Lord Jesus Christ, to the widows, the fatherless, and the hurting, to the searching and the grieving, to the broken, the helpless and the hopeless. It is my prayer that all my readers will be overwhelmed by the grace and compassion of God.

May the promises of God give you grace, peace and hope for the journey.

TABLE OF CONTENTS

INTRODUCTION

God has revealed Himself in Scripture as Creator, Sustainer, Savior, Deliverer, Ruler, Redeemer, Protector, Provider, Comforter, Counselor, Husband and Father. In each of these roles God has made promises to those who come to HIM by faith.

It is of particular interest that God makes promises to the widow, the orphan, the hurting and the needy. Throughout the Bible, God declares and demonstrates His personal care for those who are the down and out of society. God seems to take special delight in displaying His grace and power through those whom society has cast aside. (See I Corinthians 1:27-30; 2 Corinthians 12:9-10)

As I began this study, I knew that God had promised to be a husband to the widow and a father to the fatherless. What I did not know was the extent of His promises to them and to all who are struggling through harsh life experiences. In fact, just when I thought I had completed the list of references to widows and orphans, I would discover another set of verses.

The following verses make specific promises to the widow, the orphan, the hurting and the needy. This book is structured with a fivefold presentation for each Scripture reference: the promise from God, the condition upon which the promise will be fulfilled, what each promise reveals about the character and nature of God, three questions for personal growth and a prayer based on what was learned from the passage.

CHAPTER ONE

Exodus 22:22-24

"You shall not afflict any widow or fatherless child. If you afflict them in any way, and they cry at all to Me, I will surely hear their cry; and My wrath will become hot, and I will kill you with the sword; your wives shall be widows, and your children fatherless."NKJV

The Promise

God's promise in this passage is twofold. First, He promises to hear the "cry" of the widow and the orphan. The implication here is that they can simply call upon Him and He will hear their appeal with eagerness. God's promise is that He reserves special attention for the widow and the orphan.

These were the most neglected and exploited of all the citizens of Israel. Often, there was no one to look out for their needs. God promises to take up that role and be the aggressive defender of the weak.

Second, God promises that He will avenge the widow and the orphan. He describes His wrath as "hot", indicating that He is especially incensed when others mistreat the widow or the orphan. God is their special avenger and He promises to take out His anger against those who abuse them. The text indicates that God is willing to reduce those malefactors to the same status as those they have exploited.

It is almost as if God is saying, "You mistreat My widows and orphans and I will show you what it is like to be one." How appropriate that the God of Justice should take out His justice in such a way.

✷ ✷ ✷

The Condition

The only condition that God places on His special attention is that the widow and the orphan "cry at all to Me". The widow and the orphan do have an alternative to the abusive and exploitive behaviors of others. They have but to "cry" out to God and He promises to hear and to act on their behalf. To "cry" to God means to pray. Instead of complaining to the neighbors or wallowing in self-pity, the widow and the orphan are given the invitation to "cry" to God. Many who have experienced the abusive or exploitive acts of others fail to turn to God in prayer. They may complain. They may turn bitter. They may get angry. They may even try to get even. However, the best way to deal with the problem is to pray. This is true not only for the widow and orphan but also for every one of God's children.

What This Reveals About God

This passage reveals that God is a God of compassion. He has a special compassion for the widow and the orphan. Those who hurt and are vulnerable can expect that God will give attention to their special needs. He is a defender of the weak and an avenger of the helpless.

Questions for Personal Growth

1. How does it make you feel to know that God is a defender of the weak and an avenger of the helpless?

2. Since God places special attention on the widow, the orphan and the hurting, what do you expect to receive from Him?

3. Have you cried out to God for your particular needs? If not, why not?

✲ ✲ ✲

Prayer For Today

God, You have promised to be my provider, my protector and my defender. Help me not to be afraid and to put my trust in You today. Teach me how to cry out to You.

CHAPTER TWO

Deuteronomy 14:28, 29

"At the end of every third year you shall
bring out the tithe of your produce of that
year and store it up within your gates.
And the Levite, because he has no portion
nor inheritance with you, and the stranger
and the fatherless and the widow who
are within your gates, may come and eat
and be satisfied, that the LORD your God
may bless you in all the work of your hand
which you do." NKJV

The Promise

The promise in this passage is to the tither. In Israel there were three tithes that were required. The first tithe was presented to the LORD as a tithe for the support of the national entity. This tithe was brought to the temple treasury.

✡ ✡ ✡

"Bring all the tithes into the storehouse, that there may be food in MY house, and try Me now in this, says the LORD of hosts, 'If I will not open for you the windows of heaven and pour out for you such blessing that there will not be room enough to receive it." (Malachi 3:10)

✡ ✡ ✡

The "storehouse" that was mentioned here is a room in the temple to store the tithes that were brought in by the people. This tithe was to support the work of the temple and it supported the ministry of governing the nation through its priesthood.

The second tithe was for the support of the Levites and the national religious festivals. These tithes were also brought into the temple storehouse.

The third tithe was only given on every third year. It was stored within the individual cities for distribution to the Levites, the "stranger" (a foreigner), the widow and the fatherless.

God promises to bless the work and ministry of those who tithe. He invites the Levite, the stranger, the widow and the fatherless to "eat and be satisfied." This conveys full provision to meet the material needs and meaningful and fulfilling daily labor under the blessings of God.

✲ ✲ ✲

The Condition

The condition on this promise is that there must be tithes (ten percent) brought to the LORD.

✲ ✲ ✲

What This Reveals About God

Once again this reveals God special concern for those who are vulnerable. The Levite, because he had no land rights and no ability to harvest a crop or raise a herd, was included in the promise of provision. The stranger was included because of the disadvantaged status of the immigrant. The widow and the fatherless were included because they were the most vulnerable to neglect, abuse and exploitation. All these were included in God's provision.

✲ ✲ ✲

Questions For Personal Growth

1. Are you honoring God by bringing a tithe of your income to Him?

2. What would it take for God to make you "satisfied"?

3. Describe a recent time in your life when you were able to see God's provisions for your needs.

✵ ✵ ✵

Prayer For Today

Faithful God, You have proven over and over again that You will provide for all my needs. Thank You for Your personal care, Your precious promises and Your abiding presence in my life.

CHAPTER THREE

Deuteronomy 24:17-22

"You shall not pervert justice due the stranger or the fatherless, nor take a widow's garment as a pledge. But you shall remember that you were a slave in Egypt, and the LORD your God redeemed you from there; therefore I command you to do this thing. When you reap your harvest in your field, and forget a sheaf in the field, you shall not go back to get it; it shall be for the stranger, the fatherless, and the widow, that the LORD your God may bless you in all the work of your hands. When you beat your olive trees, you shall not go over the boughs again; it shall be for the stranger, the fatherless, and the widow. When you gather grapes of your vineyard, you shall not glean it afterward; it shall be for the stranger, the fatherless, and the widow. And you shall remember that you were a slave in the land of Egypt; therefore I command you to do this thing." NKJV

The Promise

God makes a promise to those who will have compassion on the disadvantaged. The stranger, the fatherless and the widow are all mentioned in the text. These were the most vulnerable of Israel's society and could easily fall through the cracks of neglect and abuse. God's blessing is promised to those who leave remnants of the harvest of wheat, olives and grapes.

During the harvesting of crops there was always a portion of the proceeds that was dropped or passed over. God commands the harvesters to leave the remnants of the crop for gleaning by the stranger, the fatherless and widow. This would allow those most needy to gather up sufficient wheat, grapes and olives to meet their requirements for daily sustenance.

✲ ✲ ✲

The Condition

It is interesting to note that God commands the Israelites to remember the days when they were enslaved. They were to consider the hardship of slavery when thinking of the needs of the stranger, the fatherless and the widow. This command to "remember" their days of slavery is seen twice in the passage. In remembering their own hardship God intends for the Israelites to show forth His compassion on those who are disadvantaged and weak. God conditions His blessing on the obedience of the Israelites to leave a portion of the crops for gleaning by the poor.

✲ ✲ ✲

What This Reveals About God

In this passage God is acting as provider and protector of both the widow and the orphan. He is acting in the role of husband and father. He demonstrates His compassion by commanding Israel to leave some of the crops for gleaning by the poor. God not only feels compassion for the widow and orphan but HE also acts upon that feeling. His compassion turns into action that HE might ensure the well being of His widows and orphans.

Questions for Personal Growth

1. In what ways are you experiencing God's compassion in your life?

2. In what ways are you showing compassion for those who are hurting?

3. Why do you think God commanded Israel to remember the days of their slavery?

✿ ✿ ✿

Prayer For Today

God of mercy, thank You for the many ways You have shown me Your compassion. May that same compassion flow from my life to others who are hurting. Open my eyes to the needs of those around me today.

CHAPTER FOUR

Deuteronomy 26:12-13

*"When you have finished laying aside all
the tithe of your increase in the third year
– the year of tithing – and have given it to
the Levite, the stranger, the fatherless, and
the widow, so that they may eat within
your gates and be filled, then you shall
say before the LORD your God: 'I have
removed the holy tithe from my house,
and also have given them to the Levite,
the stranger, the fatherless, and the widow,
according to all Your commandments
which You have commanded me; I have
not transgressed Your commandments, nor
have I forgotten them.'" NKJV*

Crushed *but not* Forsaken

The Promise

God promises that He will provide for the widow and the orphan. In this text, God commands that the third tithe be used to support the Levite, the stranger, the widow and the orphan (the fatherless). To neglect this tithe was to directly disobey God. This tithe was specifically set aside every third year to meet the needs of those who were the especially threatened of Israeli society. This provision for the vulnerable was not just a social program enacted by governing leaders; it was a command of God for His people.

The Condition

Obedience to God brings blessing. Notice verse 15 in this same passage. God commanded Israel to bring the third tithe for distribution to the most insecure of society. By making this policy into law, God was ensuring that none of the widows, strangers, orphans or Levites would be neglected.

What This Reveals About God

There are several things that we learn about God from this passage. First of all, we learn that God expects His people to make provision for those who are less fortunate. This simply means that He expects us to look out for those who are disadvantaged. Secondly, we learn that God is serious about providing for the underprivileged. He is so serious that He made it into law in Israel. This was not a voluntary offering. It was mandatory. Thirdly, we learn that God is committed to providing for the widow, the orphan, the stranger and the Levite. He did not leave it to chance. He made specific provisions for their needs.

Crushed *but not* Forsaken

Questions For Personal Growth

1. Why do you think God made it a law that Israel was to take care of the poor?

2. Name one area of your life where obedience has brought blessing.

3. Describe an area in which you are struggling with obedience to God.

✧ ✧ ✧

Prayer For Today

Father God, I do want to honor You but I sometimes struggle to obey You. Please help me to be obedient to You in every area of my life. Come and take your rightful place on the throne of my heart.

CHAPTER FIVE

Deuteronomy 27:19

"Cursed is the one who perverts the justice due the stranger, the fatherless, and the widow." NKJV

Crushed but not **Forsaken**

The Promise

This text pronounces a specific curse on those who would look on the weakest of society as easy prey. If anyone takes advantage of, abuses or otherwise neglects any of the aforementioned persons, they will be cursed by God. Here is another way in which God declares His specific protection and care for the underprivileged. In essence, God is saying, "Do not mistreat my widows, orphans or strangers, for if you do, there will be consequences."

✡ ✡ ✡

The Condition

This verse clearly states that anyone who takes advantage of a widow, an orphan or a stranger, will be cursed by God. God demands justice for these who are the most vulnerable in society. He expects His people to carefully do what is right (justice) for this group of people.

In the Hebrew language, the word for "justice", (mishpat) refers to all the functions of government and not just to the judicial processes alone. Hence, God is working to do what is right for the widow and the orphan, in every area (the judicial, the legislative and the executive branches of government). TWOT p.948

✡ ✡ ✡

What This Reveals About God

God is a God of justice and righteousness. It would be easy to take advantage of the underprivileged in Israel just as it is today. God declares that anyone who tries to profit from the misfortunes of the widow, the orphan or the stranger will be cursed.

The word "cursed" in the original language (arar) is "intended either as a judgment for misdeeds or as a deterrent to disobedience." (Mounce, p.151) God warns all those who would plan to take advantage of the widow and the orphan, that He Himself will bring a curse upon them. The weight of the curse was directly proportionate to the standing of the individual making the curse. In this case there could be no higher standing than that of the Almighty. God reveals Himself as the DEFENDER of the weak and the advocate for the abused. He is the faithful protector of the outcast.

Questions For Personal Growth

1. Describe a time when you felt truly secure.

2. Do you sense that God is your defender and your faithful protector? Do you have evidence that He is protecting you?

3. Have you thanked God for His protection today?

✧ ✧ ✧

Prayer For Today

LORD, YOU are my protector and defender. Help me rest in your protective presence. Remind me that YOU are always there to defend me and that my security comes from YOU.

CHAPTER SIX

Ruth 2:10-12

"So she fell on her face, bowed down to the ground, and said to him, 'Why have I found favor in your eyes, that you should take notice of me, since I am a foreigner.'" NKJV

"And Boaz answered and said to her, 'It has been fully reported to me, all that you have done for your mother-in-law since the death of your husband, and how you have left your father and mother and the land of your birth, and have come to a people whom you did not know before.'" NKJV

"'The LORD repay your work, and a full reward be given you by the LORD God of Israel, under whose wings you have come for refuge.'" NKJV

Crushed *but not* Forsaken

The Promise

The story of Ruth presents an awesome picture of the grace of God. She is a Moabite (foreigner) who married into a Jewish family. Her husband died and she was given the option of returning to her family in Moab. Because she had come to faith in the God of Israel, she chooses to stay with her mother-in-law, Naomi, who was also a widow.

At this time in Israel's history, Ruth has four things against her. She is a woman, a Gentile, a Moabite and a widow. But, she has found the God of Israel and HE overcomes all these obstacles with His gracious loving favor.

Naomi and Ruth were struggling just to make ends meet. This can be seen in the fact that Ruth was gleaning in the fields of Boaz. Gleaning was a practice of the Jewish people, whereby the poor were allowed to come to the fields after harvest and pick up the scraps of wheat, barley and other grains that were left by the harvesters.

Boaz acknowledges her godly character and the sacrifices she has made to remain in Israel. He blesses her for her newly found faith and dependence on the LORD. The care of God for this widow is obvious throughout the book of Ruth. His providential guidance and provisions for her are all the more gracious because she is from a Moabite background.

✡ ✡ ✡

The Condition

Ruth does not deserve the gracious favor of Boaz. In fact, she is startled by his kindnesses. We do not deserve the gracious favor of our heavenly Father. In fact, we should be startled by His kindnesses. What we see in this story is the undeserved, unmerited and unearned favor of God in the life of an alien widow.

This Moabite convert to faith in the God of Israel becomes the great grandmother of King David. She is listed in the genealogy of our Lord Jesus Christ in Matthew 1:5 and she is a picture of God's grace and compassion for the most undeserving of society.

✡ ✡ ✡

What This Reveals About God

God is portrayed in these verses as a mother hen who shelters her vulnerable chicks under her wings. (See also Psalm 17:8; 36:7; 57:1; 61:4; 63:7; 91:1,4)

God's grace and care for this unworthy widow is one of the most remarkable stories in the Bible. Not only can the widow and orphan find shelter under His wings but so can every hurting and needy person who turns to HIM for refuge.

✡ ✡ ✡

Crushed *but not* Forsaken

Questions For Personal Growth

1. List the things that make Ruth an unworthy and unexpected recipient of God's personal care.

2. What is the most remarkable thing to you in this story?

3. Where do you most feel the need for God's grace and care today?

☆ ☆ ☆

Prayer For Today

Heavenly Father, I need Your grace and care today. Open my eyes to see Your hand guiding my steps, providing for my needs and blessing my life.

CHAPTER SEVEN

2 Kings 4:1-7

"A certain woman of the wives of the sons of the prophets cried out to Elisha, saying, 'Your servant my husband is dead, and you know that your servant feared the LORD. And the creditor is coming to take my two sons to be his slaves.'" NKJV

"So Elisha said to her, 'What shall I do for you? Tell me, what do you have in the house?' And she said, 'Your maidservant has nothing in the house but a jar of oil.'" NKJV

"Then he said, 'Go, borrow vessels from everywhere, from all your neighbors — empty vessels; do not gather just a few. And when you have come in, you shall shut the door behind you and your sons; then pour it into all those vessels, and set aside the full ones.'" NKJV

"So she went in from him and shut the door behind her and her sons, who brought the vessels to her; and she poured it out. Now it came to pass, when the vessels were full, that she said to her son, 'Bring me another vessel.'" NKJV

"And he said to her, 'There is not another vessel.' So the oil ceased. The she came and told the man of God. And he said, 'Go, and sell the oil and pay your debt; and you and your sons live on the rest.'"
NKJV

The Promise

The plight of this widow is obvious from the text. She is poor, in debt and desperate. Her creditors have threatened to take her two sons as slaves if she does not pay what she owes. If the creditors took her sons to pay off the debt then she would be left with no means of support.

Creditors at this time in Israel's history were allowed to enslave debtors and their children to pay off their debts. The period of their enslavement could last until the next year of Jubilee (Leviticus 25:39-40) or until the debt was repaid.

The creditor was given guidelines about the care and treatment of all debtors in Deuteronomy 15:1-18, and they were warned about taking advantage of the destitute.

God's promise of provision for the widow can be seen in the miraculous way that the oil was sustained. There was enough supernatural provision from God to pay the debt in full and sustain the widow and her sons. Not only did they pay the debt and avoid enslavement but they also had enough left over to provide for their daily needs.

✵ ✵ ✵

The Condition

The widow in this story made a decision of faith in the midst of her crisis. She cried out to the prophet Elisha, telling him of her desperate condition. By turning to the prophet of God she was expressing her faith in the God of Israel. She knew of His promises and laid hold of His provisions. In our desperate condition we also need to lay claim to the promises of God. He is faithful and true to His Word.

✵ ✵ ✵

Crushed *but not* Forsaken

What This Reveals About God

The miracle of the unfailing oil is not only a demonstration of the power of God to provide for our needs but it also shows an important aspect of God's character. He is the God who cares for the widow and the orphan. He has active concern for the poor and the disadvantaged. He is the God who has compassion for the hurting and He is willing to do the miraculous in order to provide for their needs.

Questions For Personal Growth

1. Why do you think Elisha was willing to get involved in this widow's plight?

2. Have you seen any miracles in God's provision for your life?

3. What part did "faith" play in this story of the widow and her sons?

✵ ✵ ✵

Prayer For Today

LORD of Creation, You are able to do the miraculous. Nothing is too hard for YOU. When the hard days come, help me to quickly turn to YOU and trust YOU to meet my every need.

CHAPTER EIGHT

Psalm 10:14

"But You have seen, for You observe trouble and grief, to repay it by Your hand. The helpless commits himself to You; You are the helper of the fatherless." NKJV

The Promise

There is a threefold promise in this verse:

1. God sees our trouble and our grief. This is not simply an awareness of our condition but a careful observation of our circumstances. The idea is that God is sympathetic towards all who are grieving.

2. God promises to repay. He takes personal responsibility to see that justice and equity are carried out. He will repay us according to our need, our circumstance and our particular plight.

3. God is the identified "helper" of the fatherless. The idea here is that when our earthly fathers are no longer available, God, the heavenly Father, the Perfect parent, steps in to help. The Hebrew word for "helper" (azar) often speaks of Divine help coming in the form of military assistance but it can also mean, "personal assistance, non-military in character". God is the personal helper of the fatherless, the weak and the oppressed. [1] (TWOT p. 661)

✧ ✧ ✧

The Condition

As with all of God's promises, there is a condition. The Psalmist tells us that, "the helpless commits himself to You." There must be an act of commitment, a time of declared dependence, a surrender of self-reliance on the part of the helpless one. In other words, we must be willing to admit that we are indeed helpless and cry out to God for help. When we do cry out we can expect a ready response on the part of our God and Father for He has promised to be our "helper".

What This Reveals About God

This reveals God as the ready defender and helper of the "helpless". I have often heard the phrase, "God helps those that help themselves". This phrase implies that God is willing to do His part only when we help ourselves and have done our part. In fact, what the Scriptures teach is that God is ready and eager to help those who are willing to admit that they are "helpless". Perhaps we could rewrite the old adage to say, "God helps the helpless".

Questions For Personal Growth

1. Which part of this verse means the most to you today?

2. Do you agree with the phrase, "God helps the helpless"? Why or why not?

3. Does it help you to know that God "sees" your trouble and your grief? Why or why not?

✢ ✢ ✢

Prayer For Today

Father, I want to depend on You for everything. Help me to keep my thoughts focused on You throughout the day. Remind me that I am "helpless" without You.

CHAPTER NINE

Psalm 10:17-18

"LORD, You have heard the desire of the humble; You will prepare their heart; You will cause Your ear to hear, to do justice to the fatherless and the oppressed, that the man of the earth may oppress no more."
NKJV

Crushed *but not* Forsaken

The Promise

These verses continue the theme begun in verse 14, that is, the LORD is the helper of the fatherless. Here the promise of God is that HE will listen to the cry of the fatherless and that HE will act on their behalf. Notice the language that is used to describe this special relationship between the sovereign LORD and His humble ones.

- The language starts out by declaring this wonderful truth, namely, that God hears the desires of the humble. In this case, the "humble" are the fatherless and oppressed of Israel's society.
- The language continues to say that the LORD is intimately involved in the preparation of the heart. The idea here is that God is at work in the heart of the fatherless and the oppressed to fulfill His own purposes.
- The climactic phrase of this declaration simply states that the LORD will open His ears to hear what the fatherless and oppressed have to say. It is as if God pays special attention to the prayers of the weak.
- The Psalmist goes on to say that the LORD who has heard the cry of the poor, the fatherless, and the oppressed, will take action. This action includes ensuring justice for those mentioned in the text and ridding the earth of those who oppress.

✶ ✶ ✶

The Condition

The condition of this promise is restated throughout the Scriptures. "God resists the proud (the oppressor) but gives grace to the humble (the fatherless and the oppressed)." Humility is the attitude of heart that expresses a full dependence on God. This is the condition not only for this promise but for all promises of the Scriptures.

What This Reveals About God

Again the Bible reveals God as the advocate, champion and ally of the fatherless and the oppressed. God is the upholder of the weak and is ready to step in and defend those who humbly ask for His help. The heavenly Father is eager to support, sympathize with, and guard those that would otherwise be neglected and abused by society. The fact that God declares His willingness to hear our prayers is backed up by the statement of His intention to ensure justice for the oppressed. He is the God of judgment and justice for all who are oppressed, the fatherless, the widow and the weak.

Questions For Personal Growth

1. Are you in constant conversation with God throughout the day or just when you have a crisis?

2. Why do you think we are reluctant to ask for God's help?

3. Describe a recent answer to prayer.

✲ ✲ ✲

Prayer For Today

LORD, help me today to face whatever comes my way. Help me to have confidence in YOU. Help me to trust You even when I don't understand what You are doing. Help me to be strong and to experience Your presence.

CHAPTER TEN

Psalm 68:5-6

"A father of the fatherless, a defender of widows, is God in His holy habitation. God sets the solitary in families; He brings out those who are bound into prosperity; but the rebellious dwell in a dry land." NKJV

Crushed *but not* Forsaken

The Promise

Here is the clearest declaration in all of Scripture about God's deliberate action of being the "father of the fatherless" and a "defender of widows". Again the idea in both of these descriptive phrases is that God will take up the role of protector, advocate, sentinel and watchman over the lives of the helpless. God's first promise is to preserve, protect and defend the weak and neglected. He will be the trustee, the champion, the supporter and spokesman for those who have been abandoned as orphans or widows. He is the unseen benefactor of those whom society would overlook or discard.

There is a second promise that God gives in these verses. He states that He will set the solitary (those who have lost families, like widows and orphans) in families. This is another way of showing God's care and compassion for those who have been left in the position of being without an earthly father or a husband. In Jewish society, to be without a husband or a father was to be set on a course of almost certain want and poverty. Wicked men would often take advantage of those in this predicament.

The third promise given here is that God will deliver those who are in bondage and bring them into a place of prosperity. The text refers most certainly to God's deliverance of prisoners of war. The context of this promise leads us to make application to the widow and the orphan. God will bring them out of their bondage into freedom and prosperity.

✵ ✵ ✵

The Condition

There is a condition placed on God's promise to the fatherless and the widow. By implication, the fatherless and the widow cannot be "rebellious". Verse six states that the rebellious "dwell in a dry land." If we look at the context of this passage, there is clear reference to the exodus out of Egypt. (See verses 7-10)

Just as God faithfully provided deliverance and sustenance for the children of Israel, He will faithfully provide deliverance and sustenance for the widow and the fatherless.

In the same way, when the children of Israel rebelled, God gave them "dry land". They wandered about in the wilderness for forty years. The "dry land" was in their souls. They did not prosper spiritually. God's promises to the fatherless and the widow cannot be claimed by those who are in rebellion against HIM. All they can claim is "dry land".

✲ ✲ ✲

What This Reveals About God

We learn from these verses that our God has a Father's heart. The Father has a deep sense of responsibility for the well being of His children. When our God sees a child without an earthly father, He immediately steps in to the role once held by our earthly fathers. The only difference is that our God is PERFECT in every way. He is the perfect father and the perfect husband. He is faithful. He is caring and compassionate. He is always there for us. His love for us never fails.

Crushed *but not* **Forsaken**

We also learn that God cannot abide a rebellious child. Rebellion against God brings the consequence of "dry land". "Dry land" can be financial, physical, emotional or spiritual. In any case, God will not allow us to prosper as long as we are in rebellion against HIM.

Questions For Personal Growth

1. Does your concept of God include the fact that He is your Father? In what ways do you experience the Fatherhood of God?

2. Does your life ever feel like "dry land"? What do you do when those feelings occur?

3. What does it mean when God says that He wants you to prosper? Are you prospering? If not, why not?

✼ ✼ ✼

Prayer For Today

Father, thank you for the relationship I have with you through the Lord Jesus Christ. Help me today to know You as my heavenly Father. Give me Your peace, guide me with Your presence and keep me by Your power.

CHAPTER ELEVEN

Psalm 82:3-4

"Defend the poor and the fatherless; Do justice to the afflicted and needy. Deliver the poor and needy; Free them from the hand of the wicked." NKJV

Crushed *but not* Forsaken

The Promise

These verses carry no promise with them except the implied blessing of God. They are formed in the language of a command and they have the expectation of obedience.

✰ ✰ ✰

The Condition

When God commands us to care for the poor and needy (the widow and orphan, the downcast and outcast), He expects us to obey His command. When we obey His command we can expect His blessing. Please notice these verses in Proverbs that all speak of the necessity of caring for the poor and needy.

- Proverbs 14:21 – "He who despises his neighbor sins; But he who has mercy on the poor, happy is he."
- Proverbs 14:31 – "He who oppresses the poor reproaches his Maker, but he who honors Him has mercy on the needy."
- Proverbs 19:17 – "He who has pity on the poor lends to the LORD, and HE will pay back what he has given."
- Proverbs 21:13 – "Whoever shuts his ears to the cry of the poor will also cry himself and not be heard."
- Proverbs 22:9 – "He who has a generous eye will be blessed, for he gives of his bread to the poor."
- Proverbs 28:8 – "One who increases his possessions by usury and extortion gathers it for him who will pity the poor."

- Proverbs 28:27 – "He who gives to the poor will not lack, But he who hides his eyes will have many curses."
- Proverbs 29:7 – "The righteous considers the cause of the poor, but the wicked does not understand such knowledge."
- Proverbs 31:9 – "Open your mouth, judge righteously, and plead the cause of the poor and needy."

✲ ✲ ✲

What This Reveals About God

God's compassionate care extends beyond the widow and orphan to all those who are poor and needy. The Scriptures give us a great deal of insight into the character and nature of God when they repeatedly tell us of His concern for those who are hurting.

God is a God of justice and vengeance but He is also a God of great compassion and mercy. His care for the poor can be seen in the proliferation of commands to give to the poor, protect the poor, deliver the poor, have pity on the poor and speak up for the poor. These commands also detail the special blessings that come upon those who obediently care for those who are the most threatened in society.

✲ ✲ ✲

Crushed *but not* Forsaken

Questions For Personal Growth

1. Why do you think God placed the widow
    and the orphan in the same group as the
    poor and needy?

2. Who cares for the poor and needy of our
    society?

3. Do you believe God blesses all those who
    obediently care for the needs of those less
    fortunate?

☆ ☆ ☆

Prayer For Today

*God, You are a God of great compassion. Please help me to always
remember your promises of personal care. Help me to know that
You are there in the midst of my loneliness. Bring Your comfort to
me in those difficult days. Fill my heart with Your HOPE.*

CHAPTER TWELVE

Psalm 146:9

"The LORD watches over the strangers; He relieves the fatherless and the widow; but the way of the wicked He turns upside down." NKJV

Crushed *but not* Forsaken

The Promise

The context of this verse is a passage (vss. 5-10) extolling the righteousness and mercifulness of God. There are three promises coming from this righteous and merciful God.

First, God promises to watch over (protect) the strangers (those who are a part of Israel but are not descendants of the twelve tribes, national Israel). Today that would include immigrants and aliens.

Second, God promises to relieve the fatherless and the widow. The idea behind the word "relieve" is that of lightening the load, alleviating the stress and reducing the burden.

Third, God promises to turn the world of the wicked "upside down". In other words, God promises that the wicked will not get away with their schemes no matter how devious they may be.

✡ ✡ ✡

The Condition

This passage (146:5-10) restates the conditions upon which God's promises may be claimed. Here are the stated conditions:

- One must come to God for help. (verse 5)
- One must hope in the LORD. (verse 5)
- One must be "bowed down" or humble. (verse 8)

Again we see that God requires us to call out to HIM, come to HIM and admit that we need HIM before any help will come our way. Those who are willing to admit their need will find ready help from the righteous and merciful God. Those who are unwilling to admit their need will find resistance and opposition from that same God. We cannot set ourselves at cross purposes with God and expect to prosper.

What This Reveals About God

In all three promises of this verse, (146:9) God is revealed as the God who helps, protects, relieves and vindicates those who are in need. He is faithful, merciful and completely righteous in all He decrees.

Crushed *but not* Forsaken

Questions For Personal Growth

1. What do the words, "He relieves" mean to you? Are you feeling His relief?

2. Have you ever seen God turn the world of the wicked upside down? Why do you think He acted in that situation?

3. What part does "humility" play in our relationship with God?

✣ ✣ ✣

Prayer For Today

LORD, it comforts me to know that You are watching over me. I long to feel Your presence daily. Whenever I feel afraid, help me to quickly turn to You. Thank You for Your sovereign control over everything that happens in my life.

CHAPTER THIRTEEN

Proverbs 15:25

"The LORD will destroy the house of the proud, but HE will establish the boundary of the widow." NKJV

The Promise

Hebrew writers often used antithetical parallelisms like this one to contrast and clarify God's Word. This writing style was much like putting white letters on a black background. It gave clarity and boldness to the words. Here "the proud" is contrasted with "the widow". God promises to destroy the dwelling place of those who are self-reliant sinners (the proud) and to establish the boundary of the widow.

The implications of this promise are powerful.

First, God will intervene when wicked men try to steal the property of widows. In the Old Testament times, men of evil intent would often move the land boundary markers in order to steal property from those whom they perceived to be defenseless. What they did not realize is that God Himself promises to "establish the boundary of the widow".

Second, by extension, we can deduce that God will provide a permanent dwelling place (heaven) for the widow who trusts in HIM and He will destroy the house of the proud, consigning them to hell.

✲ ✲ ✲

The Condition

The widow must put her trust in the LORD in order to claim His promise of protection. He will only establish the boundary of those whose hope is in HIM. A self-reliant widow can only expect the same destiny as all who are self-reliant, a life of misery and ultimate destruction.

✲ ✲ ✲

What This Reveals About God

This verse reveals that God is opposed to the proud and gives grace to the humble (see also James 4:6). God is ready to stand up for the widow even so far as defending her property. He is ready to uphold and defend those who are defenseless and He will hold accountable those who seek to take advantage of the weak and needy. God is truly a God of righteousness and justice for all the oppressed.

Crushed *but not* Forsaken

Questions For Personal Growth

1. Does it give you confidence to know that God has promised to "establish" your boundary? What does this mean to you today?

2. Do you find yourself longing for your permanent home in heaven?

3. In what ways can you demonstrate your TRUST in God today?

✲ ✲ ✲

Prayer For Today

God of righteousness, thank You for standing up for me today. Some days I feel so tired that I don't think I will be able to go on. Please give me Your strength and help me to be steadfast in my faith.

CHAPTER FOURTEEN

Proverbs 23:10-11

"Do not remove the ancient landmark, nor enter the fields of the fatherless; for their Redeemer is mighty; He will plead their cause against you." NKJV

Crushed *but not* Forsaken

The Promise

The "ancient landmark" mentioned here refers to land markers or boundary lines. These markers were often just a pile of stones. To remove a landmark was tantamount to stealing land. The widow and the orphan were particularly easy prey at this point because they had no one to defend them. The promise in this passage is that their Redeemer will take up their cause. (See also Proverbs 22:22, 23 where the LORD takes up the cause of the afflicted and the poor.)

The use of the title "Redeemer" is significant. A "Redeemer" (kinsman-redeemer in Hebrew) would rescue the relative who had fallen on hard times or avenge his or her murder. The "Redeemer" is God Himself and He has promised to be the Savior of His people (the helpless, the poor, the afflicted, the widow and the orphan). (See also Ruth 2:20; 3:12, 13; 4:1-12)

✵ ✵ ✵

The Condition

This promise of protection from the Redeemer is extended to all who are needy. The specific application is to "fatherless" but the Redeemer has already declared His commitment to all who will call upon HIM. The condition is that we must abandon our dependence on ourselves and our own resources and place unwavering trust in the Redeemer.

✵ ✵ ✵

What This Reveals About God

We are reminded in this text about the LORD's role as "the Redeemer". In the Old Testament, when a family member was going through difficult days and could not see his way out, the law of the kinsman-redeemer kicked in.
Here are the three rules of the kinsman-redeemer:

- A kinsman-redeemer had to be a relative of the person who was experiencing hardship.
- A kinsman-redeemer had to be willing to help the person experiencing hardship.
- A kinsman-redeemer had to be able (financially and otherwise) to help the person in hardship.

As it applies to the fatherless in this text, God promises that He will take up the role of the kinsman-redeemer. We are told that He is "mighty". This of course means that He has unlimited power to save.

As it applies to all mankind, the Lord Jesus Christ is the perfect kinsman-redeemer.

- He is a relative in that He became a man. He became one of us so that He could redeem us from the curse of sin.
- He is willing to help us. He declared that no one took His life from Him but that He laid it down of His own will. (John 10:15)
- He is able in every way for He has all the resources of heaven at His disposal.

The Lord Jesus saw us in our desperate condition, helpless, poor, needy, afflicted, and He became our kinsman-redeemer. He redeemed us from the bondage of sin and brought us into the glorious freedom of His eternal grace.

Crushed *but not* Forsaken

✼ ✼ ✼

Questions For Personal Growth

1. Read the story of Ruth again. In what ways does Jesus act as your "kinsman-redeemer" today?

2. List three ways that God demonstrated His care for Ruth? Can these be applied to your life? How?

3. In what ways did Ruth show her faith in God while she was still a widow?

✼ ✼ ✼

Prayer For Today

LORD, You are my redeemer. Thank You for buying up all my messes, forgiving all my sins, releasing me from bondage and giving me new life. May Your amazing grace flood my heart today.

CHAPTER FIFTEEN

Isaiah 1:16-18

"Wash yourselves, make yourselves clean; put away the evil of your doings from before My eyes. Cease to do evil, learn to do good; seek justice, rebuke the oppressor; defend the fatherless, plead for the widow." NKJV

"Come now, and let us reason together," says the LORD, "Though your sins are like scarlet, they shall be as white as snow; though they are red like crimson, they shall be as wool." NKJV

Crushed *but not* Forsaken

The Promise

The broader context of these verses is a call to repentance. God indicts His people for the sins of hypocrisy and injustice. In His call to repentance, God specifically mentions the needs of the widow and the orphan. He states that part of national repentance will be the return to a demonstrated caring for those in need, the widow and the orphan.

God's promise here is really threefold:
- First, He promises in 1:18 that if there is a repentant heart evidenced by good works, there will be a thorough cleansing from the stain of sin.
- Second, He promises in 1:19 that prosperity will return and the people will "eat the good of the land".
- Third, He promises in 1:20 that continued rebellion will lead to judgment and destruction.

✵ ✵ ✵

The Condition

God's promise of cleansing and restoration is conditioned upon the true repentance of the people. The Scripture states that genuine repentance will be evidenced by a return to good works. Those good works include, but are not limited to, defending the fatherless and pleading for the widow.

Whenever God's people get right with God, there will be a return to compassionate caring for those who are needy. The Bible repeatedly states that caring for the needs of the widow and the orphan is an evidence of a healthy relationship with God.

✵ ✵ ✵

What This Reveals About God

There are at least three observations can be made about God's nature and character in this passage:

1. Notice God's call to repentance. (1:16) God so longs for relationship with His people that He calls for them to cease doing evil deeds and return to HIM. This call to repentance is based in His love and His holiness. His love longs for relationship but His holiness demands repentance.
2. Notice God's provision for cleansing. (1:18) The text uses couplets to describe the stain of sin and the effect of cleansing. Scarlet and crimson are the colors that represent the depth of our iniquity. Wool and snow, both naturally white, represent the thoroughness of our cleansing. The Lord Jesus Christ shed His blood on the cross so that we might have our sins covered, cleansed and carried away. Because of His atoning death, we can have a relationship with a holy God, knowing that our sins are forgiven and cleansed forever.
3. Notice God's prescribed compassion. (1:17) The Scripture indicates that true repentance will have a corresponding action. The evidence of genuine repentance is a return to the things that are important to God. Compassion towards the needy is high on God's priority list. God illustrates what He desires by mentioning the needs of the fatherless and the widow. If there is genuine repentance there will be genuine compassion for those who are the most at risk in society.

✲ ✲ ✲

Crushed *but not* Forsaken

Questions For Personal Growth

1. How would you describe true repentance?

2. Do you have assurance that all your sins have been cleansed and forgiven? Read Colossians 2:13-14; 1 John 1:7,9; Psalm 103.

3. Think of someone who may need to know of God's compassion. Call or write that person to assure them of your prayerful support and of God's unchanging love.

✿ ✿ ✿

Prayer For Today

Father, thank You for forgiving all my sins and giving me new life in Christ. Help me today to live out your great compassion towards the hurting people all around me. Keep me from being self-focused and guide me to a Christ-focused life.

CHAPTER SIXTEEN

Jeremiah 7:5-7

"For if you thoroughly amend your ways and your doings, if you thoroughly execute judgment between a man and his neighbor, if you do not oppress the stranger, the fatherless, and the widow, and do not shed innocent blood in this place, or walk after other gods to your hurt, then I will cause you to dwell in this place, in the land that I gave to your fathers forever and ever." NKJV

The Promise

God's promise is related to the Abrahamic Covenant in Genesis 12, 15, 17, 22. The covenant between God and Abraham was based upon the faithfulness of God and the faith of Abraham. It promised that God's people would inherit the land. The blessings of God would rest on His people in "the place" where He caused them to dwell. We all want to be in "the place" of God's blessing and here God gives a promise.

✡ ✡ ✡

The Condition

Jeremiah called for the people to amend their ways and their doings. The actions as well as the motives are in view here. Jeremiah is calling for genuine heart repentance that will be manifested in righteous living.

The promise of God's blessing is contingent upon the right heart attitude and the right treatment of others. The widows, the fatherless and the oppressed are specifically mentioned. In this passage, Jeremiah says that true repentance towards God will bear the fruit of genuine care for those who are needy, the widows, the oppressed and the fatherless.

✡ ✡ ✡

What This Reveals About God

There are several things we learn about God's character and nature from this passage.

1. God has great concern about genuine repentance. He is seeking a person whose heart is wholly toward Him.
2. God has great concern for justice (righteous judgment) among His people. He commands us to treat one another with justice and equity.
3. God has great concern for the needy, the oppressed, the widows and the fatherless. These are the ones who are most likely to be overlooked, neglected, scammed, cheated, overpowered and abused. In essence, God says, "You will know that you are in a right relationship with Me when you are caring for the needs of this group of people". He says the same thing in James 1:27.

Questions For Personal Growth

1. What does it mean to be in the "place" of God's blessing?

2. Abortion has sometimes been described as "shedding innocent blood". Has God lifted His blessing from our country because of this sin?

3. The unborn are among the most vulnerable of society. Read Proverbs 24:11-12. List three ways that you can take a stand for the unborn.

✲ ✲ ✲

Prayer For Today

Lord, You are my strength and song. Fill my heart with a fresh awareness of forgiveness, cleansing and compassion. Help me to walk in Your ways and reflect Your heart today.

CHAPTER SEVENTEEN

Jeremiah 22:15-16

"Did not your father eat and drink, and do justice and righteousness? Then it was well with him. He judged the cause of the poor and needy; then it was well. Was not this knowing Me? says the LORD." NKJV

Crushed *but not* Forsaken

The Promise

The promise in this passage is implied. God blessed Josiah, king of Judah, because he cared for "the poor and needy". The phrase, "it was well with him" carries with it the idea of wholeness and well being for him and his kingdom. God was blessing the reign of Josiah with peace, protection and prosperity.

✣ ✣ ✣

The Condition

"It was well with him" describes the blessing of God on Josiah, king of Judah, but that blessing was directly linked to his treatment of the poor and needy in his kingdom. As long as Josiah cared for the poor and the needy, he would enjoy the blessing of God on his life. If we desire God's blessings on our lives, perhaps we would do well to follow Josiah's example.

✣ ✣ ✣

What This Reveals About God

It should be clear by now that God is consistent in His call for justice towards the widow, the orphan, the poor and the needy. Not only do we see God's passionate desire for justice but we also see His compassionate care for the less fortunate. God is consistently righteous in His judgment and consistently demonstrating His mercies and His compassion on those who are hurting.

✣ ✣ ✣

Questions For Personal Growth

1. Describe one way in which you could follow Josiah's example of caring for the poor and needy.

2. The blessing of God does include wholeness and well being. How would you describe wholeness and well being?

3. Name one area of your life that needs to be made whole. Ask God to bring His "wholeness" to that area right now.

✿ ✿ ✿

Prayer For Today

Father God, You are the God of grace and mercy. You are the God of healing and forgiveness. I ask You to bring Your powerful touch to the empty places of my life. Please bring me Your wholeness.

CHAPTER EIGHTEEN

Hosea 14:3

"Assyria shall not save us, we will not ride on horses, nor will we say anymore to the work of our hands, 'You are our gods'. For in YOU the fatherless finds mercy." NKJV

Crushed *but not* Forsaken

The Promise

God declares that He will have mercy on the fatherless. Mercy is what motives the acts of compassion flowing from God's throne towards those in need.

The Condition

The promise of God's mercy is conditioned upon our seeking of mercy in HIM. In Hosea's day, the people of God had turned their backs on God and had begun to worship idols. They had actually made idols with their own hands and then bowed down and called those hand-made idols their gods. The prophet Hosea called on the people to repent and find mercy in the LORD. This is the condition that precedes the promise.

What This Reveals About God

God's character and nature are in perfect unity and harmony. Let me illustrate this principle. God is never loving without also being holy. He is never holy without also being gracious. He is never merciful without also being just. All of His attributes and characteristics operate in perfect harmony.

The Scriptures reveal that God is also consistent in all His attributes, His character, His nature and His essence. God is consistently merciful. He is consistently just. He is consistently loving. He is consistently holy. As you read through the many verses that speak of His care for the needy, you will be struck by the consistency of God's compassion on those who are hurting. Once again we see in Hosea, a God who is merciful towards the fatherless and He will be merciful to all who seek mercy in HIM.

Crushed *but not* Forsaken

Questions For Personal Growth

1. Are you aware of your need for mercy? Have you sought God for His mercies today?

2. What specific acts of compassion has God shown you during the last six months?

3. This passage reveals the tendency we all have to rely on our own resources. Is there any area of your life that needs to be surrendered to God's plan? Are you trusting in His resources today?

✫ ✫ ✫

Prayer For Today

Lord, my resources are so limited and Yours are so boundless. Help me today to rely on YOU and not on myself. May Your mercies surround me, guide me, protect me and flow through me today.

CHAPTER NINETEEN

Mark 12:41-44

"Now Jesus sat opposite the treasury and saw how the people put money into the treasury. And many who were rich put in much. Then one poor widow came and threw in two mites, which make a quadrans. So He called His disciples to Himself and said to them, 'Assuredly, I say to you that this poor widow has put in more than all those who have given to the treasury; for they all put in out of their abundance but she out of her poverty put in all that she had, her whole livelihood.'"
NKJV

Crushed *but not* Forsaken

The Promise

The promise in this passage is found in the Savior. He knew every detail of this widow's life. He saw her poverty, her need, her sacrifice and her spirit. What caused Jesus to notice this one widow out of all the people who were coming to the Temple that day? God takes special notice of the widow, the orphan, the helpless and the needy. The same Savior who sees everything and knows everything has promised to provide for our every need.

The Condition

As with the promise, the condition in this passage is implied. It is implied that the widow had a right relationship with God in that she trusted HIM completely. The widow had such faith in God that she placed "her whole livelihood" in His hands. She gave all that she had to HIM and in return He met her at her point of need.

What This Reveals About God

There are two things about God that stand out in this passage. First, it is clear that our Great Savior is all-knowing. He sees and knows everything. As Jesus watched the widow cast coins into the treasury at the Temple, He did not have to make up a story about her. He knew her story in every vivid detail. He is omniscient. Nothing surprises Him and nothing escapes His notice. Second, this same Jesus has promised to meet our every need. He used the example of the widow's sacrifice to teach His disciples a lesson about faith and giving. Jesus had full knowledge about the widow's true spiritual and financial condition and He was moved with compassion for her.

Questions For Personal Growth

1. Why do you think the widow was willing to give her last coins to the Lord's treasury?

2. What can we learn from the widow's example?

3. God knows everything about you, your needs, your hurts and your hopes. How does that affect you?

✲ ✲ ✲

Prayer For Today

Lord, You know everything about everything. You know me better than I know myself. Please give me what I need and not what I want. Prepare me for all that you have planned for me today and in the future.

CHAPTER TWENTY

Luke 7:12-15

"And when He came near the gate of the city, behold a dead man was being carried out, the only son of his mother; and she was a widow. And a large crowd from the city was with her. When the LORD saw her, He had compassion on her and said to her, 'Do not weep'. Then He came and touched the open coffin, and those who carried him stood still. And He said, 'Young man, I say to you, arise.' So he who was dead sat up and began to speak. And He presented him to his mother." NKJV

Crushed *but not* Forsaken

The Promise

God promises life and compassion for all who trust in HIM. Luke records this rather obscure passage about a widow. She had just lost her only son. The widow was without a husband and the son was without a father. The widow was probably dependent on the son for much of her livelihood. The text describes him as a man (not a boy) and so he probably worked to support his widowed mother. His death would have meant almost certain poverty for this widow. God promises His special care for the widow and the orphan and it is here demonstrated for us. The text is very specific in its declaration of Christ's compassion for the widow. How was the LORD's compassion demonstrated? He brought the dead son back to life and presented him to his mother.

✦ ✦ ✦

The Condition

There is no condition stated in the text. There is not even a mention of faith on the part of the widow or for that matter on the part of anyone present. This is simply an outward demonstration of God's special care for the widow and the orphan.

✦ ✦ ✦

What This Reveals About God

This is one of the clearest passages revealing God's special concern and commitment towards the widow and the orphan. HE hurts with the hurting and has compassion on the brokenhearted.

We must also see the power of Christ over death. Jesus raised this man from the dead. Luke tells us that there were others that were raised from the dead (7:22; 8:49-56). Death does not create a barrier for the LORD. He is LORD of the living and the dead.

Questions For Personal Growth

1. Why do you think Jesus singled out this particular widow for this miracle?

2. What changes occurred when Jesus entered the widow's circumstances? Her relationship to Jesus? Her relationship to her son? Her relationship to the community?

3. Describe what you think it means to have victory over the power of death.

✲ ✲ ✲

Prayer For Today

Father, Your presence in our lives changes everything. Help me to walk in Your victory today. May my life reflect Your presence to those You bring across my path today.

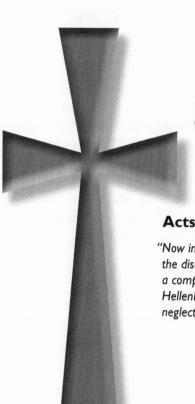

CHAPTER TWENTY-ONE

Acts 6:1

"Now in those days, when the number of the disciples was multiplying, there arose a complaint against the Hebrews by the Hellenists, because their widows were neglected in the daily distribution." NKJV

Crushed *but not* Forsaken

The Promise

God's special concern and care for the widow can again be seen in this vignette of the early church. Here is the scenario. The Hellenists (Jews from the Diaspora who were heavily influenced by Greek culture) felt that their widows were not receiving adequate food and provisions from the church.

The early church, under the leadership and direction of the Holy Spirit, appointed a special panel to oversee the daily administration of care for the widows. No other group is singled out for this special attention. God's church operating in the power of the Holy Spirit exhibited God's care for the widow.

✿ ✿ ✿

The Condition

The early church showed great sensitivity to the needs of the widow, the orphan and the hurting of society. Widows were in the local church and were being cared for by the body of Christ. For the church to experience God's blessing and the people of God to experience His power the way the early church did, there must be a concerted effort to care for the widow and the orphan, the hurting and the needy. If we are to be God's people then we must care about the things that are on God's heart.

✿ ✿ ✿

What This Reveals About God

God's Holy Spirit will always lead us in concert with the Word of God and the purposes of God. God has declared His special concern for the widow and the orphan. The church was responding to the leadership of the Holy Spirit when they directed this group of seven men to set up a daily distribution for the widows of the church. They were acting in harmony with God's declared will. This is why they experienced great power, great unity and great growth.

Questions For Personal Growth

1. Do you think that the church has fulfilled its responsibilities to the widow and the orphan? What grade would you give to your local church?

2. Are there practical ways that you can help your local church to become more aligned with God's declared will?

3. What is the relationship between God's power and God's will? Do we always experience God's power when we are doing His will? Why or why not? (Read Colossians 1:9-12)

✲ ✲ ✲

Prayer For Today

Heavenly Father, You always put us in places, situations and circumstances that will prepare us for the next leg of our journey with You. Please give me the grace and power to do Your will today.

CHAPTER
TWENTY-TWO

I Timothy 5:3

"Honor widows who are really widows."
NKJV

The Promise

This section of I Timothy goes from chapter five, verse three to chapter five, verse sixteen. The passage continues with the theme of Scripture that women who have become widowed are to be cared for by the church. God's unending compassion for widows and for the hurting can be clearly seen in His expectation that His people would show special concern for those in need. Though His compassion is implied in the text, it is most certainly underlined in the wide variety of verses from the law, the prophets, the poetic books, the historical books, the gospels and the epistles. Woven throughout the Bible is God's mercy for those in need.

✲ ✲ ✲

The Condition

The word "honor" means, "to show respect or care", "to support" or "to treat graciously". The idea here is primarily financial support but it also includes a broader definition of meeting needs. This instruction from the apostle Paul carried a caveat with it. The widow must be a true widow.

There were widows who were not alone and not destitute. Some widows had both the emotional and financial support of families. The responsibility to care for one's own household, including widows, rested squarely with the immediate family members. True widows by Paul's definition would be those who had no other means of support. They were alone and vulnerable, without the protection and support of a family group. It was to these widows that the church had Biblical mandate for "honor", "support" and "care".

What This Reveals About God

One of the things that we learn about God from this passage is that there is a dynamic tension between His sovereignty and man's responsibility. Whereas God has revealed His compassion, His mercy and His care for the widows and the hurting, He has also given responsibility to His people (whether Israel or the church) for the expression of that care. This dynamic tension can be seen throughout the Scriptures in systematic theology but it is clearly demonstrated in the very practical matters of caring for the widows, the orphans and those in need. God declares His compassion and then He requires His people to act upon His revealed character and nature. He expects us to care for those in need and to be the outworking of His compassion for the hurting.

✣ ✣ ✣

Crushed *but not* Forsaken

Questions For Personal Growth

1. List some examples of the dynamic tension between God's sovereignty (His control) and man's responsibility. (One example might be in the area of finances. God has promised to provide and yet we have the responsibility of being good stewards.)

2. Does everyone have a responsibility to care for those in need? How have you fulfilled that responsibility?

3. What role does the church play in helping people to fulfill their responsibilities to the hurting and those in need?

✵ ✵ ✵

Prayer For Today

Lord, help me to see hardships in my life as an opportunity for spiritual growth. Guide me to the best ways of expressing Your compassion for the hurting. Open my eyes to see Your hand at work in me and through me today.

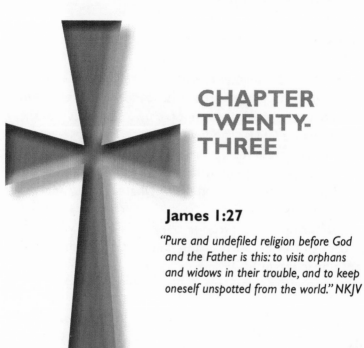

CHAPTER TWENTY-THREE

James 1:27

"Pure and undefiled religion before God and the Father is this: to visit orphans and widows in their trouble, and to keep oneself unspotted from the world." NKJV

Crushed *but not* Forsaken

The Promise

The most needy segment of the church was the widows and the orphans, those without husbands or fathers. James writes that the purest form of true religion is to show compassionate Christ-like love and care for those who are unable to reciprocate. To "visit orphans and widows" was more than just dropping by for a talk. It carried with it the idea of showing concern and doing whatever was necessary to meet needs.

God's promise to care for the needs of the widow and the orphan can be seen in this description of the lifestyle that honors the LORD.

✻ ✻ ✻

The Condition

The larger context of these verses includes 1:19-27. James is writing about the importance of being "doers of the Word and not hearers only". In other words, we must close the gap between what we know and what we actually put into practice.

James tells us that we know we are putting our faith into practice when we care for the widow and the orphan.

✻ ✻ ✻

What This Reveals About God

God's concern for the needy and His specific care for the widow and the orphan are clearly documented in Scripture.

This text reveals His expectation that His people will show that same concern. James tells us that our religion is worthless if it does not include compassionate care for those who are hurting.

Crushed *but not* Forsaken

Questions For Personal Growth

1. List the characteristics of worthless religion as outlined in James 1:22-27.

2. What are the characteristics of true religion?

3. Which of these characteristics is God wanting to build into your life?

✷ ✷ ✷

Prayer For Today

Lord, I come to You today seeking Your direction. Thank You for always being there to be my Counselor, my Helper, my Comforter, my Guide, my Protector and my Provider. Help me to express Your life and Your love to the dying world today.

CHAPTER TWENTY-FOUR

Practical Advice for a New Widow

This section of the book is reserved for practical tips and advice. The principles of God's Word will give us a foundation of spiritual truth on which to base our future. The practical tips are words of wisdom and experience to help you navigate these uncharted waters in your life.

No person plans to be a widow or an orphan. We all expect to live out our lives together with our loved ones. Sometimes the death is sudden and sometimes it is drawn out but however it happens, it leaves us in a brand new world without our loved ones.

It's a terrible thing to have to say, "I am a widow". It is just as difficult to have to say "I" or "me" instead of "we" or "us". Here is a list of practical things that have helped others manage life after the loss of a loved one. These tips are primarily for the widow but can also be applied to anyone who has recently experienced the loss of someone dear. These are practical things that you can do to take care of yourself physically, emotionally and spiritually.

1. Begin taking a multi-vitamin that has B complex, C and E. The stress of losing a loved one creates a major drain on your system. Replacing those vitamins and minerals will help your system to cope with the stress.

2. Get more copies of the death certificate than you think you need. There may be copies required a year or even two years after the death of your loved one. The cost of getting copies later can increase dramatically.

3. If you work and have direct deposit on your paycheck you may want to stop the direct deposit for a while. You will need money and the bank might freeze the account on the death of a spouse.

4. When you are notifying everyone of the death, you may want to type up a form letter with the full name, address, date of the death and your relationship to the deceased. Make copies to send out. One of the places you will mail this letter is to the credit card companies. If the credit card was in the name of the deceased, destroy the card and tell the credit card company that you have done so.

5. Get a spiral notebook and keep track of every person and company you have contacted with the date of the letter or phone call and a brief summary of what was said.
   - You will need to do this because your memory will come and go during the early stages of the grieving process.
   - Write down the name of the person you talk to, the date and the time. Write down what they tell you. If you have to call them again you will

have a record of your conversation. It will help you to get better results faster.

6. Notify the life insurance company and the employer immediately so that benefits can be processed.

7. Your appetite, eating patterns, sleep patterns and thought processes can be foggy and somewhat disconnected. This is also a normal part of the grieving process. Be sure to contact your physician if these disruptions become unmanageable.

8. You need nourishment. The stress demands on your body will require that you get some nutritious meals. There will be days when you don't want to eat and don't feel like eating.

9. Try to eat breakfast even when you don't feel like eating. Fruits and whole grain cereals are important for your body now more than ever. Yogurts will also help replace vital bacteria in your system.

10. Herbal teas can help with the evening hours and ease you into a night of rest. Nightmares often occur during the grieving process and if they do it is better to get up and read Scripture or read a good book. Lying in bed and fretting will only make things worse.

11. Your tendency during the grieving process may be to neglect your personal appearance and hygiene. As with many times in your life, a good long hot shower or bath will do wonders. Getting a new haircut, a manicure or a new outfit can change the focus of the day.

12. Uplifting praise music can be a great source of comfort and it can also remind you of the faithfulness of God through your loss.

13. Don't be in too big a hurry to make major decisions about the house, where you will live, what you will do, how you will manage. We almost never make good decisions when we are grieving, depressed or discouraged.

14. If you receive an insurance settlement, put it in the bank in a savings or money market account and just wait for a few months before you make any decisions about what to do with the money.

    • During the early stages of the grieving process your mind may be scrambled. It is better to have your money earning a small interest rate than to make unwise investments and end up with no funds for the future.

    • When you are able to focus and think more clearly you will be able to make better decisions about what to do with your money. Don't do anything until you have talked with a trusted friend or counselor.

15. Talk to your pastor about the grieving process and ask him and others to keep you in prayer.

16. Talk with other widows and gain insights from their experiences.

17. Call the local hospital and hospice to find out about grief support groups. This is an invaluable resource in helping you cope. If you go to a grief support group and feel that it is just too much, too early, you can always get up and walk out. Everyone there will understand. Every person grieves at their own pace and in their own way. These groups have been extremely helpful for others and you might find them helpful in your grieving as well.

18. Beware of the many scams and con artists that are looking for an easy mark and want to take advantage of your disorientation. Talk with a trusted friend, pastor or counselor before you make any purchases.

19. After a few months you may want to talk with a financial planner. I recommend contacting Crown Financial Ministries for help. Crown.org is their web site and they can be a great resource for your financial decisions.

20. An accordion file that has alphabetized dividers is an excellent way to keep track of paperwork. You will be surprised by the amount of paperwork that comes your way. This is an easy way to keep track and not let loose papers pile up or get lost.

21. Be aware that some people cannot talk about death. Some of the people you consider close friends may avoid you because they do not know how to talk about death. It is not that they don't love and care about you, they just don't know how to deal with it and so they avoid it all together.

22. There will also be people who will be there for you no matter what. When you need help, ask for it. Car repairs, a fallen tree, a broken fixture, a plumbing problem or any physical need will give others an opportunity to help you. Give them the opportunity to do something practical to help. You will be blessed and so will they.

23. Depression is one of the stages we go through during the grieving process. Because depression is so common among those who have lost a loved one, I wanted to include here some advice from a trained grief therapist. Every day you should do these three things:

- First, do something for yourself. This can be something as simple as a walk in the park, a manicure, a haircut, a new outfit, a new hobby or a new book.
- Second, do something for someone else. Write a note, make a call, take a meal to someone, visit someone who is sick or do some selfless act of service for someone in need.
- Third, get out of the house and go somewhere every day. (Even if it is only to the grocery store) Your tendency will be to close yourself off and just hibernate. If you do this you will feel more and more depressed.

24. Realize that some days you are just going to cry a lot. You may find yourself crying without even knowing what triggered it. Crying is part of the process of grieving. Give yourself permission to cry. Keep a small package of tissues with you. They really do come in handy.

25. Many widows say that nights and weekends are the worst. It is a good idea to schedule something to do on the weekends (household chores, laundry or cleaning) so that you are not just sitting around thinking about how bad things are for you.

26. Exercise is a real help to your physical and emotional health. Walking for 30 minutes a day will reduce stress, improve circulation, and release chemicals into your system that promote overall health.

27. Plan something to look forward to. Put it on the calendar and anticipate the event. This might be a trip, a cruise, a planned lunch with a friend, a visit to someone you haven't seen for a while, an excursion to the museum, a concert or a public garden.

28. Consider learning a new skill, a new language, a new hobby, or a new friend. Your local public school system probably has an adult continuing education program that will offer many courses in a wide variety of fields. Most programs and courses are offered at night and on the weekends (the very times that you want to be doing something). The costs associated with these courses are minimal.

29. Learn to go to the movies alone and learn to go out to eat alone. It will seem strange at first but you will get used to it and you might even enjoy it after a while. There are some real advantages to being alone. You don't have to be on anyone's schedule but your own. You don't have to concern yourself with anyone's wishes except your own.

30. Some people may tell you not to make any major decisions for a year. This is an arbitrary number and it will be different for some people. Just don't get in too much of a hurry. Most decisions don't have to be made instantly and so you can wait. Time is a great healer and your thinking will be clearer in time. You will be more focused and better able to make good decisions about yourself and your future.

END NOTES

1 Archer, Gleason L., Harris, R. Laird, Waltke, Bruce K., _Theological Wordbook of the Old Testament_, volume 2, Chicago: Moody Press, 1980, pp. 1123

2 Mounce, William D., _Mounce's Complete Expository Dictionary of Old and New Testament Words_, Grand Rapids: Zondervan, 2006, pp. 1316

6862738R0

Made in the USA
Lexington, KY
28 September 2010